T0160909

SOJOURNS

POEMS OF
LIFE AND LOVE

KATHRYN CAROLE ELLISON

Published by Lady Bug Books, an imprint of Brisance Books Group.
Lady Bug Press and the distinctive ladybug logo are registered trademarks of
Lady Bug Books, LLC.

Lady Bug Books
400 112th Avenue N.E.
Suite 230
Bellevue, WA 98004
www.ladybugbooks.net

For information about custom editions, special sales and permissions, please contact
Brisance Books Group at specialsales@brisancebooksgroup.com

Manufactured in the United States of America
ISBN: 978-1-944194-21-5

First Edition: April 2017

A NOTE FROM THE AUTHOR

The poems in this book were written over many, many years...
as gifts, of sorts, to my children. I began writing them in the
1970s, when my children were reaching the age of reason and
as I found myself in the position of becoming a single parent.
I needed something special to share with them—something that
would become a tradition, a ritual they could always count on...

And so the Advent Poems began—one day, decades ago—
with a poem 'gifted' to them each day during the December
holiday season every year. Forty years later... my children still
look forward to the poems that started a family tradition
that new generations have come to cherish.

It's my sincere hope that you will embrace and enjoy them
as we have and share them with those you love.

Children of the Light was among the first poems I wrote and
is included in each of the *Poems of Life and Love* books in
The Ellison Collection: *Heartstrings, Inspirations, Celebrations,
Sojourns, Awakenings,* and *Sanctuary.* After writing hundreds
of poems, it is still my favorite. The words came from my
heart and my soul and flowed so effortlessly that it was
written in a single sitting. All I needed to do was
capture the words on paper.

Light, to me, represented all that was good and pure and right
with the world, and I believed then—as I do today—that those
elements live in my children... and perhaps in all of us.
We need only to dare...

– KCE

DEDICATION

To my parents: Herb and Bernice Haas

Mom, you were the poet who went before me...
unpublished, but appreciated nonetheless.

And Dad, you always believed in me,
no matter what direction my life took.
Thank you for your faith in me,
and for your unconditional love.

TABLE OF CONTENTS

LIFE'S JOYS

LIFE'S LESSONS

LIFE'S GIFTS

LIFE'S JOYS

LIFE

Life is a sojourn – usually taken alone –
During which you perfect your soul,
So that on the day that you are recalled
You'll learn if you've reached your goal.

The journey may be hard, but remember this:
You were not born knowing it all.
Survive each day and you will succeed,
Picking yourself up after each fall.

The goal is to perfect your soul for God,
Done by learning from each step as you go.
You learn from your suffering to be content;
And bask in the glow of goodness as you grow.

The contentment you seek will bring you peace,
And a return to your lost perfection.
You will not rest until you've found
Your path and your true direction.

HAPPINESS IS A CHOICE

Don't go to the end of your life with regret
That true happiness was, for you, out of reach.
Staying stuck in old patterns and habits is a choice,
Just as happiness is your *choice*. (So I preach!)

Comfort of the familiar permeates our lives,
And fear of change overrides happier endings.
We pretend to others and to ourselves
That we're content with what life brings.

But deep within, the desire to laugh properly,
And to let childlike silliness enter your life again,
Should be your goal. Practice it every day!
Smile and be happy. You don't need to explain!

FRIENDSHIP

Peace on earth begins with you,
And the one who bugs you the most.
It's amazing how much you learn each time
You go with him to the post.

If he is always "bugging" you,
Check for "termites" in your own house.
By removing your own annoying quirks
You have less cause to grouse.

If you set out to understand another,
As you travel through each doorway;
It's amazing, but true, you'll reap great rewards,
Understanding yourself along the way.

No one is perfect, but should you insist,
You'll experience great resistance.
Take your chance on an imperfect friend;
It's the *only* kind in existence.

CHILDREN OF THE LIGHT

There are those souls who bring the light,
Who spill it out for all to share.
And with a joy that does excite,
They show the world that they do care.
It is so very bright.

In this sharing, love does pervade
Into their lives and cycles round;
And as this light is outward played
The love is also inward bound.
It is an awesome trade.

You are a soul whose light is shared.
It comes from deep within your heart.
It's best because it is not spared,
Because it's total, not just part.
And I am glad you've dared.

CELEBRATING CHANGE

There's not a tomb big enough to hold all the bones
Of the parts of ourselves that died along the way,
As changes were necessary for our very survival...
To live our lives; to face another day.

All changes have a melancholy, even those we desire,
According to Anatole France, a French novelist.
What is left behind is a part of ourselves,
But we must die to one life before another can exist.

With every new stage of life there are changes
To grieve as well as to celebrate.
We are constantly passing from one state to another,
And we're sent guides and mentors to light our way.

Andre Gide, another French novelist.
Said this about change (and more):
"Man cannot discover new oceans
(Without) courage to lose sight of the shore."

Your life does not get better by chance.
Your path is not prearranged.
Even if you stumble, you're moving forward.
Your life gets better by change.

No one can go back and make a new beginning,
It's water under the bridge, as they say.
But anyone can make a new ending,
By starting on the path today.

Live Now

"Live now, believe me, wait not till tomorrow,
Gather the roses of life today."
A French man, Ronsard, spoke those words.
He, indeed, had a lot to say.

Now is all there is, the future's not here,
And the past is far behind us, and gone.
If we could remember to live in the present,
Then to our minds we would not be a pawn.

Let today be yours. Live in the now.
Take time to live before time takes you.
Never put off till tomorrow – do it today,
Keep the magic in *now* – make it new!

Make your plans as if you would live forever –
And tread the earth for at least a thousand years.
But walk as if you'd take your last step today.
It is a wise program for living, my dears.

Just do your best with the tools you have
And you will gain so many more,
As you go along life's interesting paths,
And open to yourselves each new door.

Boomerang blues – or bliss?

Australia does not have exclusive hold
On 'boomerang' effects, as lives unfold.
In our own lives our actions can rebound
With accuracy that can be most profound.

Our words, our deeds and our thoughts, as well,
Upon return, can make our life hell;
Or they might have an uplifting effect.
It quite depends on what we direct.

In the game of life we should expect
Exactly what we give – it's most direct.
The precision can be astonishing –
Can make you cry or make you sing.

Sincerity

When pure sincerity forms within,
It is outwardly realized in another's heart.
The words need not even be spoken,
But the message is pure, right from the start.

Sincerity is impossible unless it pervades
The whole being with thoughts, words, and deeds.
The pretense of it saps your foundation of character.
Make sure you're being sincere before you proceed.

Sincerity is always effective and honorable;
It's also much easier than commonly supposed.
Sincerity and competence is a strong combination.
Your success will most likely not be opposed.

A GOOD GROUP

No Roman candles, no shooting stars
(Except those on the Fourth of July)
In day-to-day business as usual mode.
(Read on. I'll amplify.)

A good group is always better, by far,
Than a spectacular one, any day.
When leaders become like superstars,
Their egos often get in the way.

Few superstars are down-to-earth.
Their fame demands more fame.
When full of themselves they cannot lead;
They change the rules of the game.

They often fly off and sometimes crash,
Leaving the group without lead.
The best leader, by far, is one who has
No fragile ego to feed.

The wise leader settles for good work first;
He lets others have their say.
Give me a leader whose ego is intact,
And do it without delay.

THREE STEPS TO SUCCESS

To know success that is worthwhile
You must take steps, and there are three.
Take them in order and you will see
Success will make your entire being smile.

The first step is not hard at all;
It's simply to begin the thing –
To jump right in – get in the swing.
Hopeful feelings do enthrall.

The next part is not nearly as fun;
It's called the struggle, and takes toil.
It means your fingers will know the soil.
But that's how victories are won.

Most people drop out at this stage;
They can't accept life as it is planned.
It's fair, though, and the goal is grand.
Your life's worth to you is your gauge.

At last the final step – the third
In French it's known as 'tour de force,'
Conviction and hard work your source.
In victory you have the final word.

LIFE'S LESSONS

THE BLAME GAME

Anger is a passion that is all-consuming;
It poisons your thoughts and your senses.
Right actions get tabled and madness prevails.
You overreact to any outside offenses.

Preoccupation with this burning rage
Tamps down your growth, that's for sure.
It makes you second-rate people, you know,
And incredibly immature.

The contributions you were meant to make
As citizens of the universe
Get sidelined by this quite opposing host –
This anger makes matters worse.

Soon blame starts creeping through the cracks:
("It's surely their fault, not mine.")
And others' faults become your focus.
The whole thing's quite asinine.

You know that blaming is a dead-end road,
And not the best tool for growing.
If you let go of blaming and anger,
Your positive energy will keep flowing.

TACT-ICAL WISDOM

Never start a sentence with the words, "No offense..."
It's almost always followed by the word "but..."
And what follows is almost always guaranteed
To bring on a rash of words you'll wish to rebut.

Wisdom is knowing when to speak your mind;
And also knowing when to mind your speech.
Consider the interpretation of your words;
And your intent before you speak, I beseech.

We are all masters of our unsaid words.
As well as slaves of the words we let out.
Tact is the art of making your point
Without making enemies along your route.

It is tact that is golden, not silence after all.
Tact, indeed, is a kind of mind reading...
The ability to describe others as they see themselves.
It's with the intelligence of the heart you are proceeding.

TOOLS FOR LEARNING

When you were young, say two or three,
A world of risks was yours for the taking.
You approached each risk without benefit of committee
And you worried not about mistakes you'd be making.

You got back up and tried the stunt again
And failed, or else succeeded to completion.
You didn't fuss much; you didn't complain;
Your ego didn't seem to face depletion.

The years have passed and you're now "mature."
A fear of looking foolish if you try and fail
Will prevent your growth; you'll feel insecure;
You'll be on your path of self-betrayal.

Remember, your mistakes are learning tools.
Without them there'd be little growth at all.
Be gentle with yourself; and play the fools,
And know that mistakes do not bring downfall.

YOUR ROLE ON LIFE'S STAGE

What role in life have you selected for yourself ?
And in what style are you going to play it?
Divine Will has a hand in assigning our role,
But choices we make can weight it.

Some of us will act in only a short drama.
And for some, the performance will be long...
The roles we accept must be played to perfection.
If it's difficult, remember, complaining is wrong.

Wherever you find yourself in your life's role
Give an impeccable performance. Do your best!
Whatever your role, play it with all your might.
Enjoy your life! In yourself, invest!

DISCRETION

Discretion is reason, raised to perfection;
It's a guide to us all in our duties of life.
Discretion of speech is more than eloquence,
And important in relationships to avoid strife.

Nothing is more dangerous than a friend without discretion.
A prudent enemy may be preferable. Are you surprised?
You wouldn't tell your enemies all of your secrets
But with an imprudent friend, your trust is compromised.

Discretion and censorship are not in the same league.
Censorship is considered an act of omission.
No, discretion is knowing what to say, and when...
Stay true to your purpose, and fulfill your mission.

Wisdom teaches you when to use your discretion...
When to share your feelings, your thoughts, and with whom.
Having two ears and one mouth, it would stand to reason...
We should listen twice as much as we speak, I assume.

LEARN SOMETHING NEW

Learning something new
Is a goal to set each day.
Being more 'at home' in the world
Is a wonderful way to stay
Alive and eager to share
Your knowledge and your thoughts.
Learning also can remove
Those tired old 'shoulds' and 'oughts.'

'Cause life is like playing a solo
In public before you know
The instrument or the music –
You simply learn it as you go.

So many sources for learning,
Everywhere you look –
Magazines and TV,
And also from a book.

More recently, computers –
Just log on, type a title, and read,
The information seems endless;
It downloads at breakneck speed!

Being with others is another way
To learn something you don't know.
To attend a public lecture,
Put yourself in the car, and go!

CHANGE BECOMES VISIBLE

When inner changes do occur
Or when transition comes about
The visible manifestation of this shows up
In two situations, it turns out.

In love and in work are the places most clear
That change is seen to have occurred:
The first serious love of a person's life,
Where one is truly, completely enraptured;
And the first long-term job with an eye to the future,
And an attitude mature and devout.

In youth one plays and tries all the ways
Of dealing with life on life's conditions.
Little by little the lessons are learned,
Sometimes after a few repetitions.

Roles are adopted and then tossed out
When found to be utterly deplorable,
Until the time you find the ones
That seem to be potentially explorable.
The way you deal in these new roles
Is the birth of your very own traditions.

Evolution

Not a force, but a power... not a cause, but a law:
Evolution requires the management of change.
Your evolution occurs mostly through your behavior.
You innovate new behavior and adapt; an exchange.

The best place to start this evolution of all things
(For evolution takes place all around you, as well)
Is through the imagination needed to adapt.
If you can think it, you can do it – that's it in a nutshell.

There are those who will argue for creationist theory,
(It was all created in six days after it had begun)
But the theory of evolution is as open to doubt
As the theory that the earth revolves around the sun.

There are no shortcuts in the evolution of all things.
"Time takes time" are the words to remember.
Evolution is a tinkerer, spurred by imagination.
It never looks to the future, live now, be a member.

Failure guides evolution, nothing is perfect.
But successes provide incentive for improvements, for gains.
You are the facilitator of your own evolution.
Those who do not move do not notice their chains.

LONELINESS

It's possible to feel lonely in a crowd;
You feel you don't belong.
Just check sometimes on how you are feeling
When it seems that something is wrong.

To be lonely is to be aware
Of an emptiness down deep inside
That takes more than people or things to fill it.
Within you your answer resides.

Even the person you love most in the world
Cannot satisfy this need.
To know that you can't rely on another
Can sometimes make your heart bleed.

Maybe in the end it is you that you're missing;
That You that's connected to All.
Some call it God, of which you're a part.
Break through that self-imposed wall.

And when you find your path to self,
Just watch your spirits soar.
At long last you become who you are;
And then you're lonely no more.

THE CUMULATIVE EFFECT

We are but what we have cumulatively become,
Filled with experiences and actions through the years.
Some experiences have been wonderful, taken us right to the top,
While others may have left us in tears.

That's the way life is, and your actions do count
More than you might ever have thought.
What you do through your life always has consequences.
Some are positive and beautiful, and some are not.

As observed by others, your life might be defined
By your actions, by your friends, by what you say.
That reputation is really all you have
To carry you as you go along your way.

It's your choice. Be helpful and pleasant and kind;
Be sincere; and always keep your word.
The opposite path of action could only bring you grief.
Your life would always be in discord.

When thinking of your future and trying to plan it
The confusion can put your thoughts in disarray.
Remember, the years will always take care of themselves.
Your responsibility is to take care of each day.

DEFINING YOURSELF

Are you so busy living your life day to day
That you don't ask yourself about your pathway?
"What kind of person do I want to be?"
Is one question to put to yourself, you see.

And, "What are my personal ideals as I live?"
"Whom do I admire?" "What is my objective?"
Write down in a journal your list of traits,
Then practice them daily, do not vacillate.

It's time to stop being vague about your goal.
Without attention to it, you're only playing a role.
Decide, then practice, who you want to be,
And be that person most certainly.

LIFE'S EXPERIENCES

Life is filled with difficult experiences;
One might seem harder than the next.
They occur for reasons unknown to you;
They were not written in any text.

They become the crucibles that forge your nature,
Your values, your beliefs, your truth.
They often occur when least expected.
They've continued since your youth.

They develop the internal powers and freedom
Needed to handle life with grace.
You gain strength and courage and confidence
To meet life head on, face-to-face.

PATIENCE

Patience is not simply the ability to wait.
No, it's how you behave while you are waiting.
Patience will always achieve more than force.
The rewards will surpass what you are anticipating.

The keys to patience are acceptance and faith.
Accept things as they are in the world around you.
Have faith in yourself and the direction you have chosen.
To pursue your goals, you must continue.

Patience is not rebelling against each hardship.
It's simply waiting till it passes, and keeping your hope.
Patience, persistence and perspiration bring success.
It's not out of reach, it's within your scope.

Patience and perseverance have a magical effect,
Before which obstacles tend to vanish.
They are the best remedy for every trouble.
You'll be amazed at what you are able to accomplish.

When you master your patience, you master everything else.
It's the key to it all as you watch it unfold.
You only get the chicken by hatching the egg,
Not smashing it... Now, you've been told.

DATES ON A TOMBSTONE

From whom much is given, much is expected,
And you've been given more than most:
Your brains, your charm, your common sense,
And your compassion for others foremost.

If your life doesn't seem to be working out
The way you envisioned it might,
You have the responsibility to search until
You find the approach that is right.

Confidence begs to be followed, you know,
(Because you've always been leaders)
If anything at all is important to you,
Then it's important. That's all; no impeders!

No matter how great your life's going for you
There are always new chapters to explore.
Jonathan Winters once said: "If your ship doesn't come in,
Then swim out to it." Meet life, I implore!

There will be two dates on your tombstones,
And all of your friends will read 'em
But all that's going to matter is
That little dash between them.*

* Last verse attributed to Kevin Welch.

PROCESS IS PROGRESS

Process is defined as a continuous action,
Or a series of changes in a definite manner.
That means constant movement throughout your lives,
Wherever you may wander.

Life must flow through you all of your days.
You're a receptacle, a conduit with a wide range.
Learning is a lifelong process you pursue
To keep abreast of change.

The good life is process, not a state of being.
It's a direction, not a destination.
Life is a lively process of becoming,
While digesting new information.

It's also a process of determining what doesn't work,
Then disentangling from it and finding a new way.
It's watching your patterns and learning from them,
Then correcting them to go on another day.

In the long run you shape your lives and yourselves.
The process ends only at death.
The choices you make you are responsible for,
And you live with them till you take your last breath.

The most difficult thing is the decision to act.
The rest is tenacity for staying on the trail.
You can change and control different facets of your life.
The process is the reward. You cannot fail.

Finding your identity is through work and through love.
(Both imply giving rather than getting.)
Stay in the process, don't think of success,
And you'll have a lifetime with no regretting.

THE DOUBLE-EDGED SWORD

Sometimes when we try to do
What we think is the very best thing ... for us
We run into barriers that seem so high
And in our struggle, create... a fuss.

We worry and fret, but forge on ahead
Creating havoc and in short... a stir.
And then we find, upon breaking through
Our position was much better off... where we were.

Does this happen to you? It has to me,
When my ego needed massaging... for uniqueness.
At the time I felt I was the only one
Who fought to overcome... this weakness.

But then I found that in my struggle
To overcome an imaginary foe... me,
My uniqueness – like the struggle itself –
Was only an attempt to break... free.

All along I was free, but didn't know it.
It turned out to be struggle for its own... sake.
It taught me there was a quieter way
By which to spring free and that is to... "take."

Take hold of the freedom that is yours at birth
As soon as you become aware... of its glory.
How you grab it and how it becomes yours
Is merely a chapter in... your story.

One's ego is a wonderful thing.
It's both necessary and totally... useless.
To know the degree to which it can help
Is not much more than a simple... wild guess.

We keep on trying; it's the nature of Man
To pick himself up from the dust... and go forth.
We learn from our mistakes, it is said.
We do these things to test... our innate worth.

ENDURANCE

Endurance is patience that is concentrated.
Heroism is endurance for one minute more.
Endurance is critical if you want to succeed
At whatever is before you; and furthermore…
Endurance always precedes success,
Building character and strength by the score.

Wondrous is the strength of cheerfulness,
And its power of endurance.
The cheerful person will accomplish much more,
And do it better. His jubilance
Will buoy him up to do a better job
Than someone who shows reluctance.

Struggle begets strength; like the proverbial diamond
That is coal before it is squeezed with pressure.
All bad fortune can be conquered by endurance.
It's the spirit that can bear all things. You will endure
Beyond any pain or struggle you might experience.
The sky is not your limit... you are!

LIFE'S GIFTS

ACCEPT UNCERTAINTY AS A BLESSING

The only thing that is certain, my dears,
Is that change will occur in spite of you.
With change comes uncertainty. Oh my, yes,
Throughout your life it will ensue.

Uncertainty is a blessing in disguise
Though it may not bring you any peace.
But by believing the miraculous might happen to you
Your wonder and awe will never cease.

Do yourself a favor the next time you're asking
Why and how, when and where... and even who.
Don't look for the answer, just ride the wave,
And it will undoubtedly come home to you.

HOLD DEATH CLOSE

Death is by no means separate from life;
It is present in all that we do.
We all interact with death every day;
As a subject it should not be taboo.

We taste death as we might taste a very fine wine,
Feeling its keen edge now and then.
In life's disappointments and trifling losses
It's present again and again.

As a dancer might hold a partner by the hand
A death is held in every separation.
A delicate balance as we walk the fine line
From birth to the last emigration.

ART

Literature – demands we pay attention.
We freeze the moment in the frame
Created by the author's words,
Seeing it in its particularity
Beyond its nameless status quo,
And wonder at the awe of it.

Paintings – ask for our participation.
The painter frames the face and asks
That we look deeply through the eyes,
And see all faces for all times;
That we *look*... deeply beyond what's framed
And really see what's in the space.

Music – clamors in our ears,
Measuring the time span between the notes
And asks us to listen well,
And hear beyond the music played
To sounds from deep within the earth
And sounds of our own silences.

ART... a frame around a moment
That makes us stop and look and hear.
We learn to know the world as it is
And all that dwells therein is real.
Through art we learn to know ourselves
And we connect with holy things.

THE ESSENCE OF FAITHFULNESS

Life is an ordered and elegant whole
That follows easily comprehensible laws.
It is not a series of random episodes
Which, when connected together, can give you pause.

Essence of Faithfulness lies in holding opinions
That are correct while regarding the Ultimate.
Remember that Divine Order is fundamentally good,
And intelligent, as through life you navigate.

Divine Will exists and directs the universe
With justice and order and goodness.
Fix your resolve on expecting these three,
And as they unfold, you'll bear witness.

Trust there is Divine Intelligence at work
Whose intentions direct the universe.
Steer your life in accordance with this order:
The results will provide nothing adverse.

When you strive to conform your intentions
And incorporate Divine Order into your life,
You won't feel persecuted, weak or confused
Or resentful with your circumstances. There's no strife.

Instead you'll feel strong, purposeful and sure.
You'll accept events with intelligence and grace.
Shun the things that are not in your control.
You will dwell in a happier place.

Faithfulness is not a blind belief.
It's the antidote to bitterness and confusion.
View the world as an integrated whole.
Divine Will exists for our inclusion.

TURNING POINTS

The turning points along your path
Are marked by loss of direction.
For what you took for granted once
You now must seek out correction.

In nature, growth involves vast change.
The eggshell cracks, the nest must crumble;
The tadpole's tail will always fall off.
The scope of change makes you humble.

For humans, the signs are not as clear
When transition occurs without warning.
Disorientation seems to be the norm,
Until you can experience a dawning.

To cope with change, you grasp at straws,
And repeat old familiar acts.
You need to see from new perspectives,
So as to learn a new set of facts.

What's learned is that transition is
Set in motion by an ending.
You must learn to let go of outdated things
To accept the new ones pending.

Confusion abounds in the middle of it all.
What identified you once, now does not.
What has ended will ultimately be replaced,
But the wound is a tender spot.

Following all forms of mass confusion
You can make a brand new start...
A new beginning that sets you free
To follow your own heart.

PAIN

When friends are in pain and ask for help
Just be there... to empathize.
The more they suffer, the less you should say.
A concept that is difficult to internalize.

Feel another's pain as he shares his story,
Enough to keep him from going under;
But not so much that you both drown.
That would be, on your part, a blunder.

It's good to laugh and share happy times
With friends who entertain,
But you've never truly been with another
'Till you've been with him in his pain.

Listen carefully to, and be there for,
Your friend when he's feeling weak.
You know the pain of the other person
When *their* tears run down *your* cheek.

ON THE DEATH OF MY HUSBAND

He died by inches,
Leaving only his shell,
And then the wind
Blew that away.
And he was gone forever.

Childhood fears became
Larger than life itself.
Pulling into his shell
Became the only safe place
To maneuver through life.

I hope that somewhere
His spirit is dancing a jig,
And partying like
There's no tomorrow.
I hope his spirit is happy again.

TO LIVE IS TO CHANGE

Change is always for the best
Although you may not agree.
Without it things would remain stagnant
And die, every human and tree.
For a conscious being, to exist is to change,
And to change is to mature.
To mature is to go on creating
Yourself, in all you endure.

In your art and in daily living;
In your work and in your play,
There's always room for improvement.
There's always a better way.
The trick is to flow with each step
And not try to skip one or two.
The last step always builds on the first,
And you are creating you.

To live is to change, there's no disagreement;
The facts are there in plain sight.
And to live well is to have changed often.
It is our natural birthright.
Perfection is a goal to keep in mind.
Why else would we change and try again?
The joy is in the pursuit as much
As it's in the prize we obtain.

Reflection

Legs once strong, now barely shuffle.
The movement is painstakingly slow.
The once quick response of clever one-liners
Lie in his throat, lost in the shadow.

A lover once, we filled our lives
With friends and travel and joy.
An entrepreneur with business success:
Many people he did employ.

Till the sickness came, slowly at first...
The signs? It was difficult to spot then.
A forgotten moment – we all have them –
A name, a shared memory forgotten.

Fast forward in time, the symptoms increased
To include getting lost, and forgetting the bath.
Our relationship changed to patient and nurse.
Our shared life no more, each on a different path.

The house reeked of loneliness, though we were together,
Him in his world, one I could never enter.
He railed at me for pulling away,
When in fact he was heading to his own small center.

Inch by inch he left the world,
Dying a little with each hammer blow.
And with it the daily routine shifted
From boldness to anger, and then to sorrow.

TRANSITIONS

You've heard of the proverbial straw, I'm sure,
That put the camel in traction...
Compare it, if you will, to the chain of events
That brought on your own changing action.

Each single event was probably not
The determinate transaction –
Yet transition occurred each step of the way,
Like with the camel, a cumulative reaction.

Transition begins at one place in your life,
And its effects are seen from every angle.
Your positive mindset gives you all you need
So that, from old tapes, you disentangle.

Soon you find yourself reaching farther and farther,
Adopting methods that to you are 'newfangled.'
The effects of this change reach deep within
And emanate out to every quadrangle.

A CLOSING THOUGHT

POETRY

It's the revelation
Of a sensation
That the poet
(Wouldn't you know it)
Believes to be
Felt only interiorly
And personal to
The writer who
... **writes it.**

It's the interpretation
Of a sensation
That was fueled by
A poet's sigh
And believed to be
Shared mutually
And personal to
The lucky one who
... **reads it.**

About the Author

Kathryn Carole Ellison is a former newspaper columnist
and journalist and, of course, a poet.

She lives near her children and stepchildren and their families in the
Pacific Northwest, and spends winters in the sunshine of Arizona.

You might find her on the golf course with friends, river rafting,
writing poems... or at the opera.

Late Bloomer

Our culture honors youth with all
It's unbridled effervescence.
We older ones sit back and nod
As if in acquiescence.

And when our confidence really gels
In early convalescence...
'We can't be getting old!' we cry,
'We're still struggling with adolescence!'

ACKNOWLEDGMENTS

I have many people to thank...

First of all, my children Jon and Nicole LaFollette, for inspiring the writing of these poems in the first place. And for encouraging me to continue my writing, even though their wisdom and compassion surpass mine.

My wonderful stepchildren, Debbie and John Bacon, Jeff and Sandy Ellison, and Tom and Sue Ellison, who, with their children and grandchildren, continue to be a major part of my life and are loved deeply by me. These poems are for you, too.

Eva LaFollette, the dearest daughter-in-law one could ever wish for... and one of my dearest friends. Your encouragement and interest are so appreciated.

My good friends who have received a poem or two of mine in their Christmas cards these many years, for complimenting me on the messages in my poems. Your encouragement kept me writing.

To Kim Kiyosaki who introduced me to the right person to get the publishing process underway... that person being Mona Gambetta with Brisance Books Group who has the experience and know-how to make these books happen.

And finally, to John Laughlin, a fellow traveler in life, who encourages me every day in the writing and publishing process. John, I love having you in my cheering section!

OTHER BOOKS

by Kathryn Carole Ellison

AWAKENINGS

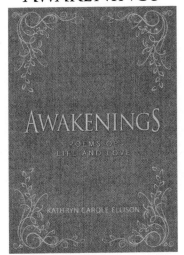

SANCTUARY

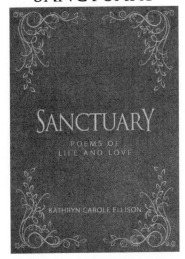

HEARTSTRINGS

INSPIRATIONS

CELEBRATIONS